HOW 100 DANDELIONS GREW

written by
Louisa Ernesto

illustrated by
Franklin Ayers

HARCOURT BRACE & COMPANY

Orlando Atlanta Austin Boston San Francisco Chicago Dallas New York
Toronto London

One little seed went riding on the wind. It went up and down.

Then it fell to the ground.

One dandelion plant began to grow. The leaves grew up, and the roots grew down.

Up popped a yellow flower.
It opened in the day,
and it shut at night.

One day the flower turned
into a soft, white ball.

Along came a boy.

Whoosh!
Then 100 little seeds
went riding on the wind.